I0617062

100 Mindful Moments to Balance and Energize

A Holistic Guide to Self-Care and Inner Strength

By Wade Brill

Beacon Hill Productions

100 Mindful Moments to Balance and Energize

Copyright © 2025 by Wade Brill

All rights reserved. No part of this book may be reproduced, distributed, or transmitted in any form or by any means, including photocopying, recording, or other electronic or mechanical methods, without the prior written permission of the publisher, except in the case of brief quotations embodied in reviews and certain other noncommercial uses permitted by copyright law.

For permissions, inquiries, or bulk orders, contact:
https://wadebrill.com/connect

Beacon Hill Productions

Print ISBN: 979-8-9928868-0-1
e-book ISBN: 979-8-9928868-1-8

Printed in the United States

Cover design by Tom Moss
Interior design by Tom Moss

This book is intended for informational and inspirational purposes only. The author and publisher make no guarantees regarding the application of the practices discussed. Readers should consult a qualified professional for medical, psychological, or therapeutic advice.

The mindfulness practices and insights shared in this book are inspired by both ancient wisdom and modern research. While the concepts may not be entirely unique, they are presented through the author's personal lens, experience, and methodology.

First Edition: April, 2025

Dedication

To my loving mother

who taught me how to

"just breathe"

Intention

This book is designed to inspire and empower
you to slow down and embrace
intentional practices that bring balance
and vitality to your life.

. . . .

When you nurture yourself holistically,
you unlock the energy and passion to pursue
what lights you up and become a radiant source
of love and stability in the world.

Contents

. . . .

Introduction

Taking care of myself was a necessity. At the age of 21, I was diagnosed with Hodgkin's lymphoma. As I endured the taxing early weeks of chemotherapy, I also bore witness to my mother's battle with leukemia—one she ultimately lost. We were both treated in the same hospital. Only a few floors separated our experiences. As I watched my mother pass away, a mirror of my own mortality and the preciousness of life glimmered in my face.

Life is delicate, beautiful, messy and amazing. Our time on Earth is pretty uncontrollable. We never know why our loved ones fade or why illnesses happen quite when they do. So much of life is beyond our control, yet we hold incredible power in how we care for ourselves and the conscious choices we make.

I know the weight of feeling powerless. When I was diagnosed with cancer and forced to cut short my study-abroad adventure, I felt like my life had been hijacked. The whirlwind of stress—the lump in my neck, the endless tests and procedures, and the flood of terrifying emotions—felt insurmountable. But even in the chaos, I discovered a choice. I could crumble beneath the weight, or I could pause, slow down, and mindfully focus on how to care for myself. That choice became my anchor, keeping me grounded amid the storm.

I realized my mind, body, and soul craved something deeper: holistic support. I needed space to breathe fully, pause to process, feel my emotions, and reflect. I longed to let go of unhelpful thoughts and discover a sense of ease. Self-care evolved from a checklist into a way of being—an energetic transformation.

I examined the clutter and priorities in my life, cut out toxicity, and elevated what truly nourished me. I deepened my meditation practice. My journal became my closest confidant. I set boundaries, tuned into my body's intuition, and redefined my relationship with food as a form of medicine. I became intentional about how my environment and community affected me. These practices weren't luxuries; they were lifelines. Without prioritizing my well-being, I wouldn't have had the energy or resilience to keep moving forward. Life was already chaotic, messy, and overwhelming—I couldn't make drastic changes. With little money and limited resources, I focused on small, sustainable shifts that made a big impact. These practices built my muscles of grit and confidence, empowering me to keep pursuing my dreams, even amid the storm.

The 100 mindful moments in this book are tools that I learned, practiced and created during treatment and after healing from the emotional and physical after-effects of chemotherapy and losing my mother. I took the time and space to recognize how I care for myself as a holistic being, integrating my knowledge as a Professional Certified Coach, Pilates instructor, meditation teacher and foodie. This book is a collection of tips based on how I mentally treated myself, what I fed myself, the way I moved my body, the space I surrounded myself with, and how I renewed my energy. Practicing these self-care tips became the core element of my life. They helped me to prioritize self-care, so that I could have a strong foundation that gave me the energy to live my life and do what I love.

The Mindful Hand of Self-Care

The Mindful Hand of Self-Care model (Figure 1) emerged from the 100 tips covered in this book. Each finger of your hand symbolizes an essential principle of self-care, which makes them easy to remember.

Your thumb represents your mindset. Your opposable thumb gives you the ability to grip and make things. This is the same with your mindset. A lot of your work with self-care begins in your mind and with the thoughts you create and feed.

The pointer finger represents fuel. You use your pointer fingers to point to the things you want, to what looks good and to what you want more of.

The middle finger represents movement because if you're like many people, this is typically the first thing that gets ditched when life gets busy.

The ring finger represents space. This includes the people, places and items with which you surround yourself.

The pinky finger represents renewal. It's likely you often forget about resting and renewing your energy, just like you largely ignore your pinky fingers.

When you can collectively bring awareness to each finger, each mode of self-care in micro-moments of pause, you will feel more embodied, grounded and present. This allows you to show up more powerfully for other people and the world.

Space

Anything and everything you let into your personal space. From people, to objects, to places and things. Your home, desk, closet or car. Think about light, clutter, smells, design, etc.

Movement

Refers to consciously moving your physical body in any way, shape, and form.

Fuel

How to think about food in relationship to supporting your energy levels. What you consciously decide to put in your body.

Renewal

How much do you rest and recharge your batteries? Sleep, relaxation, quiet time, meditation, creative time, bubble baths, massages, journaling, etc.

fig. 1

Mind

Refers to your self-talk, mental chatter, and emotional responses. The voices of fear that hold you back and the whispers of doubt that keep you frozen from making choices.

Self-care is one of the most proactive deeds you can do for yourself. It is not selfish, it is smart. Building a daily self-care practice creates a seatbelt that will help protect you during life's bumpy and unexpected potholes. It will sustain your energy a lot more than an annual yoga retreat or vacation.

To start, pick a tip a day to practice mindfully. Take the time to notice how much more energy, attention and enthusiasm you have for life and the world around you as a result.

Slowing Down Helps You And The World

How often do you catch yourself saying, I want to go to the gym today or I want to have time for a creative hobby, yet these practices are the first items to get ditched on your list of priorities because of lack of time? And yet, at the end of the day you feel guilty for not taking action on practices that matter most to you.

This is American culture. We praise busyness. Anything in the category of self-care, slowing down or wellness is seen as overly indulgent and not productive. However, I am here to take a stand. To be a voice of reason in our overstimulated and saturated world. If we as a human race don't slow down to be more mindful about how we take care of ourselves, how can we have compassion for others or even the environment? Learning to practice self-care is like watering our own plant. The plant needs to stay hydrated and nourished so that it can give off oxygen and clean the air. If the plant isn't watered, it will shrivel up and not be able to participate in our ecosystem.

According to the World Health Organization, The COVID-19 Pandemic caused a 25 to 27 percent increase in the prevalence of depression and anxiety around the world. Stress in America, according to the American Psychological Association highlights how the Nation is recovering from collective trauma, which is negatively impacting the population's well-being. The data demonstrates that adults ages 35 to 44 reported an increase in their mental health diagnoses from 31% reported in 2019 to 45% in 2023. Adults ages 18 to 34 reported the highest rate of mental illness at 50% in 2023. The American Psychiatric Association's 2024 mental health poll highlights that 43% of adults say they feel more anxious than the previous year due to current events. These data points highlight the profound influence of societal systems and current events on mental health, underscoring the urgent need for collective action to support well-being.

As much as we need to work to change policy and untangle the unhelpful beliefs that have become embedded in culture, we as individuals also get to play an active role in our own health and well-being. We get to take mindful moments throughout the day to come back to ourselves. To come back to the present moment and make conscious choices. Choices that get to serve us and the greater collective. Engaging in self-care helps you to build more curiosity, self-empathy and self-compassion, which can open you up to sensing our collective human experience more richly.

Additionally, I can share with you that, as someone who identifies as a sensitive soul, establishing self-care practices became essential to managing my own energy. Honoring my sense of self helped me to withstand the urge to people-please or abandon my own needs. My hope for you is that this workbook helps to nourish you, so that you, too, can give more powerfully to the world.

How To Use This Book

This book is intended to help you create space that will inspire you to pause and care for yourself. This way you can show up for the world feeling and being your best.

Keep this book by your nightstand or in your favorite self-care space in your home. Turn to it daily and take a mindful moment.

Step 1. Think about which finger of the Mindful Hand of Self-Care you feel you want the most support in, right now.

Step 2. Flip to that section and read through the tips in that category. Select one that stands out to you. Create your own if nothing quite fits!

Step 3. At the end of each chapter, use the journaling section. It will help you to get clear about how you want to incorporate this tip into your day.

Step 4. Reflect on your mindful moment practice and integrate your learnings into your life.

Step 5. Celebrate yourself for taking action and prioritizing your well-being. Snap a picture of you doing your practice and share it with a friend or co-worker via social channels or a text. Let's always remind each other that practicing self-care is smart, not selfish.

Step 6. Revisit this book when you are ready to engage in your next mindful moment and repeat the above steps.

What thoughts do you create?

—

"If you wanna fly,

you got to give up the shit

that weighs you down."

- Toni Morrison

Mindset

The power of your thoughts directs where your energy flows. Unplug from the busy and overstimulated world and tap into the richness of your awareness. In these moments of pause, you can create space, grow and unlock insights that help decrease stress and anxiety.

Explore the power of your thoughts by taking a mindful moment.

Self-care begins in the mind. How you talk to yourself is the essence of how you construct your reality and the relationship with yourself. When the mind is full of fear, self-doubt, 'should's and guilt, you can feel physically and mentally weighed down.

Your energy gets stagnant. Unhelpful thoughts cloud your thinking and prevent you from showing up in the world available to connect and be present.

Before my journey into chemotherapy began, I felt the weight and spiral of my thoughts create a wind of anxiety. The pulsating energy of New York City throbbed inside my body as thoughts of: "What if chemotherapy doesn't work?" "What will I look like with no hair?" The fear of losing my life dangled in my face. With my first taste of chemotherapy, I knew it was going to take a lot of will-power to get myself into a better state of mind. Not long after chemotherapy began, I lost my mother to complications with her leukemia, which only deepened my gaze inwards.

Looking back, I realize that being so young and vulnerable and faced with many life interruptions simultaneously, forced me to discover, listen to and befriend my internal voice. Slowing down to pay attention to how I was mentally treating myself was key to managing anxiety and stress. I felt iso-lated in my experience. Not only was I going through chemo and I couldn't relate to any of my friends, but my siblings and I had just lost our mom and were all mourning in our own ways. I was profoundly alone that I couldn't afford to be at odds with myself—I had to find solace within. It was at this moment that I realized, my well-being is up to me. I get the opportunity to be my best friend instead of my worst enemy.

I started a consistent journaling practice every night before bed, where I would word-vomit my day, my emotions, and my thoughts onto the page and truly get to hear and connect to the layers of myself. My journal became my best friend: she traveled to various coffee shops around town, and I would even bring her with me to chemotherapy. My journal was a place for me to express myself fully and unapologetically. I recognized patterns in my internal dialogue. Beliefs, assumptions, and expectations were limiting me from letting go and healing.

After a few months of lingering in my dark space, I woke up to a choice point. I could stay in my rabbit hole of negativity and gloom or start to find the silver lining and lesson in everything that was happening. I choice the latter mindset. My desire to self-soothe and heal during this trying time inspired me to explore the power of gratitude, breath, my *monkey mind*, and to unearth the limiting beliefs that were holding me back.

I also deepened my morning meditation practice. This was a safe space where I could hear the underlying thoughts and emotions below the surface of a loud mind. Meditation supported me understanding how I relate to my thoughts and listen to my body's wisdom. After six months of a consistentish morning meditation practice, I was able to be curious with the anxiety in my body instead of judging or avoiding it. The tightness in my chest and throat softened—releasing the reactive vibration that pulsed in my cells. Meditation helped me to slow down and ask myself, "what is here to pay attention to?" I had the capacity to listen and tend to the spectrum of emotions and insights present.

One of the greatest gifts my meditation practice gave me was space—a profound sense of mental clarity and freedom. Instead of being weighed down by an endless tangle of thoughts, I discovered the power to choose which ones deserved my attention. Picture your mind as a desk buried under endless stacks of paper, each sheet representing a thought clamoring for your focus. The clutter feels suffocating, overwhelming, until you begin to pause, witness, and accept each sheet. With each acknowledgment, the papers are sorted and filed away, creating room to breathe. My mind didn't calm down because the thoughts vanished, but because they were recognized and organized, leaving me with a sense of peace and order.

In this chapter, I invite you to get curious about your thoughts and feelings. What is your relationship to the thoughts in the mind? What beliefs linger below the surface? What stories do you hear? What's the tone of your internal voice(s)? In what ways do you slow down to acknowledge the thoughts in the mind?

The following tips are ways I created mindful moments successfully to manage my mental self-talk and chatter in various aspects of my life.

Remember, self-care begins with the thoughts you create.

Pause Before You Peek

Instead of reacting to cell phones every time they vibrate, take three deep breaths. Allow technology to *support you*, instead of it consuming you. This pause allows you to be in control rather than respond to a potentially anxiety-causing stimulus.

Be Your Best Friend... Not Your Worst Enemy

When feeling sad or sluggish, tell yourself: "I love you," and bring compassion to the moment. Repeat the words to yourself in your head or say it out loud in front of a mirror. You can even try giving yourself a physical hug. Drop the negative chatter and treat yourself with love and kindness—just as you would treat your best friend.

Get Out of Your Head and into Your Heart

Any time your mind gets trapped by analysis paralysis, snap out by opening up and acting from your heart. Acting with more love and kindness will always steer you in the right direction when making a decision.

Check Your Routine

Pause to explore the habits you have created. Are they truly yours or have you learned them from someone else? What can you let go of that doesn't support you? Journal out what you discover.

Future in Focus

Instead of allowing your mind to constantly question your choices and decisions-distracting you from the present, schedule time into your week or month to pause and review. Celebrate where you went and how far you've come. Acknowledge what you learned and highlight where you want to go. Trust that setting aside this time to plan for the future will help you let go of the worries in the now that suck your focus.

Brain-Dump

Sleep soundly at night by de-cluttering the noise in your head.
Keep a notebook by your bed and write down thoughts that are keeping you
up. Watch the thoughts flow out of your mind and into the universe.

Turn Fear into Frontier

Push your comfort zone every day and discover the beauty of the new
frontier and all you can do. You know you are close when that sense of fear
and the unknown tickles in your belly. Consciously step forward with those
sensations and let them give you strength versus holding you back.

Just Breathe

In moments of panic or anxiety, come back to your breath. Breathe in
for the count of 5 and out for the count of 7 to slow down your mind and
body. If the thought doesn't serve you, let it go and rest your attention
on your breath.

Mental Shift

Instead of looking at what is wrong and not working, shift your mentality
by discovering the lesson, the prospect or the insight in the scenario.
Opportunities are all around us. We get to be open to find the light of
wisdom and the lesson learned.

Busy Bee

Is your mind constantly scheduling your next move? Are you running through
your day, crossing off your checklist but forgetting to be present where
you are? If so, that mental chatter will eventually make you feel burned and
whipped out. To prevent overdoing it, pause and place your hand over your
heart. Let the warmth and weight of your hand slow you down, bring you
back to the present moment and find the calm amid the storm.

Quiet Your Monkey Mind

When your mind starts to chatter and "What ifs" arise, quiet the voice by gently labeling the thought as a "thinking trap." Release what doesn't serve you, and come back to what is true in this moment, such as your breath or a pleasant object in your space. Anchoring into the present moment is key to quieting the *monkeys in the mind*.

Pressure Cooker

Don't let time pressure make you feel busier than you already are. Take a moment to breathe and enjoy the journey between your scheduled appointments. Trust that everything will get done and you will be where you need to be.

Hear It. Feel It. Write It.

When your mind creates stories, says cynical words or gets in the way of being you, take a moment to kindly acknowledge the voice, feel it in your body, get curious and let it go by writing it down. Keep track of these thoughts, and by writing it down, you can eventually free yourself from this pattern.

What Do You Hear?

Recognize whose voice you hear in your head. Is it a family member? Boss? Best friend? Notice what words they say and when they say it. Ask yourself if their voice is supportive or not? Remember that you always have your own inner wise voice and choice of what you want to listen to.

Power of Your Words

We sometimes forget how much power the words we say affect our well-being. Words such as *have to*, *should* and *need to* are constantly used to describe the daily activities we perform. Instead of feeling trapped or imprisoned by your language, feel inspired and own the actions that you *get to take*.

Ground Your Feet in Gratitude

When you first roll out of bed, place your feet on the earth and ground yourself with a sentence of gratitude. Let that energy be the foundation for your day's flow.

Shut It Down

Your thoughts are powerful and can spark a swirl of anxiety. Shut off the mental overwhelm of worries by placing the tip of your tongue on the roof of your mouth. That is an acupuncture point that connects the pituitary and pineal glands, and this action reduces mental chatter.

Turn FOMO into MOFO

Instead of having social media FOMO (fear of missing out), let social media inspire you to be MOFO (mindful of future opportunities). Let your thoughts connect you to people, places and things you love instead of making you feel jealous, angry, inadequate and fearful of missing out.

Snap a Pic

When you catch your mind spinning out of control - feeling overwhelmed and anxious - take out your phone and snap a picture of any bit of nature. Take a moment to acknowledge life around you and snap a picture of the sunrise, a flower on your desk or a fly on your window sill. Let that picture interrupt your thought pattern and slow your world down to put everything into perspective.

Reflect to Connect and Direct

Each morning, pause to connect to your top three values by writing them down. Start your day by directing your energy towards what you want to create so that you can have focus and vibrant energy throughout your day.

Space to Create
Your Own Mindful Moments

Journal Prompts — *Pick your practice.*

What *mindful moment* tip feels most aligned with your needs right now?

Why is practicing this tip important for you?

What about this tip gets you excited?

When do you want to commit to starting this practice? (Date, Time, Let's go!)

How do you imagine feeling while you practice this tip?

What is one tangible result you are hoping to create?

Pause to process.

What is one thing you are celebrating about yourself?

What stood out to you as you engaged with this practice?

How did this tip influence your energy, mood or mindset?

What's one insight you want to carry forward?

What are you grateful for in this moment?

What are you putting into your body?

—

"Take care of your body.

It's the only place you have to live."

- Jim Rohn

Fuel

In order to keep us moving, living, being and breathing, our systems require nourishment, substance, energy and power. The variety of nutrients and the type of food we ingest matters and affects how we show up in life. Each of our bodies digests and processes food differently, affecting our bodies' natural rhythms for better or for worse.

Explore these tips to learn how you can fuel yourself from the inside out.

Fuel is about the gasoline I choose to put in my vehicle. It is the nourishment that powers my cells and keeps me moving, being and doing. Growing up, food was centered around family, entertainment and celebration. We had family dinner almost every night with a balance of meat, vegetables, carbs and salad. When I was bored, I would mindlessly grab an Oreo or cup of Goldfish to munch on before dinner. Even though I was genuinely a healthy eater, I veered towards the "see-it diet." Meaning, if I saw it, I ate it. There wasn't much room for discernment. However, my connection to my body and how I fueled it changed dramatically when I was going through chemotherapy. Receiving a bi-weekly dose of poison into my bloodstream made me more aware of what was happening to my body on a cellular level. Meditation gave me the ability to tune into the sensations of my body, and to listen to it. I noticed what type of foods made me nauseous and what types of fuel my body craved. I felt my body yearn for clean fuel to support my healthy cells. I craved so many vegetables and was excited by the fact that the more nutrient-dense food I consumed, the healthier my cells were. Food became a type of medicine I could use to feel strong and energized.

I learned how to cook for myself at this time. I didn't have a mom to wait on me or make sure I was eating properly. Instead, I was empowered to listen to myself and develop these skills on my own. I played around with tips and tricks of how to food shop and meal prep on a budget. I learned how to clean and cut different vegetables, how to cook roasted vegetables and how to prepare meat and beans in a variety of ways. Luckily, I come from a family of foodies so I knew the genes to cook well were somewhere inside of me, I just had to tap-in.

My relationship to my body, and how I chose to nourish it, transformed from an act of entertainment to an act of service and gratitude. I viewed my body as a temple and wanted to send more love and kindness to every cell at every opportunity (again, this goes back to the concept of becoming my best friend versus my worst enemy.) I honored the cravings of my body and listened by enjoying and not overindulging. I never restricted my body from what it craved to feel well-fueled. I would have muffins and cookies if my body wanted them, but I ate them with full awareness so that I could savor each bite instead of scarfing them down and feeling guilty about it. Just as my meditation practices taught me how to listen to my thoughts, it also helped me listen to my body and learn to decipher how eating different types of food affects my energy and how I feel.

Post-chemotherapy, my love for nourishing my body continues to morph and grow deeper. The food I cook and eat isn't just about powering my cells with nutrients, but it feels like a spiritual gesture to express my values of love, creativity and connection. Talking about food, cooking, eating, trying and sharing food brings me joy. Food inspires my senses, connects me to my body and the earth that grows our food. With every bite, I pause to notice what part of my body am I fueling. Am I eating this cookie to feed my heart? Am I eating this sandwich because my stomach is hungry? Am I reaching for cereal because I am feeding a need for entertainment? Listening to the various physical and emotional cues support me building a kinder relationship to my body and well-being.

I invite you to get curious about your relationship to food. While growing up, what were your family's norms around food? How did your relationship to fueling your body change over time? What inspired you to learn how to cook and food shop? When you fuel your body, what values do you emphasize? What feels pleasurable about the act of nourishing yourself?

The tips that follow are inspired by how I used fuel to nourish my sacred temple back to health as well as how I continue to feel healthy and strong. Use what feels supportive below and allow it to spark creative ways you can mindfully nourish yourself.

Wake Up Your Insides

First thing in the morning, hydrate your body from the inside out with a glass of water and fresh lemon. It not only purifies your system, but it also awakens your taste buds and senses.

Eat 5 Varieties of Vegetables a Day to Keep the Doctor Away

You are what you eat. Get your variety of nutrients and energy from quality produce. Keep it interesting, fun and nutritious by eating a variety of colors and textures. Use this tip while at salad bars, planning your shopping list or ordering food.

Fuel Yourself

Pack a lunch and healthy snacks the night before to help keep your energy, hunger and emotions in balance. Take leftovers, or get creative by compiling a balanced meal with the ingredients in your fridge. Do it the night before so you aren't scrambling in the morning.

Power 3x3 Plus Fat

Meal planning and food prep gets to be a fun, creative and efficient way to keep yourself and your bank account in balance. When creating your grocery list, think of 3 different types of vegetables, 3 different types of protein, 3 different types of carbs and some healthy fats. Using this method helps you build a variety of yummy and healthy *Buddha bowls* that never get boring and always taste satisfying.

Sit & Chew

Even if you are rushing out the door, busy at work or starving when you come home, sit while you eat to chew each bite. Sitting and chewing around thirty times helps aid in digestion. Focus on how much more satisfying your meal will taste when you can eat it with full presence.

Pack a Snack Before a Hanger Attack

Avoid getting hangry [hunger+anger]. Don't leave home without a bag of nuts, a piece of fruit or a healthy pick-me-up to keep your energy and mood in balance. Homemade energy balls are my favorite satisfying snack to carry around.

Beat Peer Pressure

Order water with lemon at Happy Hour instead of an alcoholic drink. Lemon tastes great and makes your drink look fancier. Don't feel like you need to drink just because others are. Stay hydrated and listen to what your body wants. Focus on how much better you will feel by staying committed to your intention.

Eat With Intention

Ask yourself what part of you is hungry: eyes, mouth, hands, heart, taste buds, tongue or stomach? Eat with purpose and awareness to reduce excessive or unnecessary snacking.

Fresh and Freeze

Keep yourself in balance by baking your own sweet treats and snacks instead of buying packaged foods that are filled with gross ingredients. Freeze what you make so they stay fresh longer. You are also less likely to over-indulge when they are out of sight and out of mind.

Chew Don't Swipe

When eating alone, focus on chewing, not your cell phone or screens. See if you can resist the urge to multi-task and stay out of the internet wormhole. Direct your attention to the sensation of chewing. When you give your full attention to your meal, research demonstrates you end up eating less because you are able to notice the fullness and hunger cues from the gut to brain.

Create a Mealtime Ritual

Create a ritual before the start of every meal to help you transition into the present moment. Whether it be saying a sentence of gratitude, feeling the warmth of the bowl, thinking of someone you love or simply feeling your feet on the ground. Pause with full awareness so that you can be present and fully appreciate your meal. You will be surprised how this practice makes your meals more satisfying and aids portion control.

Potluck Dinner with Friends

Food always tastes better when you are with company. Instead of dining at extravagant restaurants every time you want to connect to your friends, try planning a fun, themed potluck–for no holiday-related reason. It is a great way to practice your cooking skills, get creative, eat healthier, be more intimate and save some pennies.

Ignite Your Senses with Fresh Ingredients

Buy fresh produce, protein and herbs. Notice how eating fresh, organic and grass-fed products connects you back to the earth and makes you more conscious of what you feed yourself. Notice the difference in taste and how your body digests it.

Cook with Love

While you cook, cook with the mantra of love. Each chop, mince or stir gets to be an act of love. Appreciate the process of cooking and remember that each bite you are feeding yourself and others is pure love that helps you feel strong, keeps you breathing and gives you energy.

Meditate While You Chop

Cooking is a great mindfulness practice. Wind down your day by chopping veggies in bite-size pieces so they are easier to chew and digest. Notice how much more connected you are to what you are eating.

Balance in Your Basket

When food shopping, make sure your basket has a balance of color, proteins, vegetables, fats and carbohydrates. Switch up your weekly purchases because your body craves a variety of nutrients that you won't get from eating the same meal over and over.

When the Sweet Tooth Hits

Eating a treat doesn't have to be filled with guilt and shame. If you want sugar, look for the most unprocessed type--sugars like maple syrup or raw honey. Slow down to savor the taste so you can recognize when you have had enough. Try to not eat it fast and pretend it never existed. Be proud and be loud about what you savor.

Be Adventurous

Escape the cooking rut of eating and preparing the same meals over and over again by picking up a mystery product at the grocery store. Cook up a new interesting vegetable, piece of protein or anything else that looks exciting! Thanks to the internet, you can Google the perfect recipe or check out the mindful cooking inspiration on Centered in the City.

Veggie Spaghetti

Get your vegetables in by eating them in the form of pasta! Have fun turning nutritious and delicious vegetables into spaghetti by using a spiralizer. Top your veggie spaghetti with your favorite sauce and add some protein to create a healthy balanced meal. The texture and taste will keep you full and satisfied without feeling heavy or bloated.

Restaurant Anxiety

When ordering food, don't let the price of your meal options cause anxiety. Order what your body craves and take home half of it. This way you save money, practice portion control and never restrict your body from what it wants. You also get to enjoy your social life without overthinking or breaking your budget.

Space to Create
Your Own Mindful Moments

Journal Prompts — *Pick your practice.*

What *mindful moment* tip feels most aligned with your needs right now?

Why is practicing this tip important for you?

What about this tip gets you excited?

When do you want to commit to starting this practice? (Date, Time, Let's go!)

How do you imagine feeling while you practice this tip?

What is one tangible result you are hoping to create?

Pause to process.

What is one thing you are celebrating about yourself?

What stood out to you as you engaged with this practice?

How did this tip influence your energy, mood or mindset?

What's one insight you want to carry forward?

What are you grateful for in this moment?

How are you moving your body?

—

"To keep the body in good health is a duty...
otherwise we shall not be able to keep our
mind strong and clear."

- Buddha

Movement

In this section, explore personal tips that help you take care of your physical body. Your body is the precious vehicle that allows you to move, eat, explore and connect to the world around you. When we forget to move our bodies, we make it harder for ourselves to be productive and fully participate in our world.

Learn how to incorporate movement into your everyday self-care plan.

I used to be pretty lazy when I was younger. I enjoyed watching TV while my whole family went to the gym, swam, ran or did yoga. I was not into it. It wasn't until I was in high school that I discovered how good it felt to move my body, to sweat and feel strong.

My fitness journey began like most people's does. I used the elliptical or I walked on an incline on the treadmill. Weights, intense cardio, and group classes intimidated me. I didn't fall in love with the gym until I found Pilates. Pilates was the gateway to strengthening my mind/body connection. My first Pilates class transformed the way I connected to movement. Pilates challenged my mind/body connection to wake up my core, lengthen my muscles and work towards moving and using my body from my power-house. Having deeper strength in my bones made me feel like superwom-an. Since sophomore year of high school, movement has been a daily ritual. I was never into high school sports so I had the opportunity to explore other fitness modalities that helped me connect to my breath, my body, my mind and my inner strength.

During chemotherapy, I discovered how hard it was to build and maintain muscle. The toxicity and potency of chemotherapy ate away my muscles, so I focused on restorative postures in yoga and cardio to help flush my lymphatic system as well as sweat out the chemicals. I remember taking a spin class and having a unique smell seep out of my pores.

It's so distinct and ingrained in my memory. The best way I can describe it is a sterile BO-body odor mix with hand sanitizer. Adding physical fitness into my regime while going through chemo was one of the ways I could help support my body to heal and thrive. I felt empowered knowing I was doing the best I could to help my body restore and release from the inside out.

Experiencing chemo allowed me to tune in deeper to the knowledge and wisdom of my body. Making sure I had movement in my daily flow created a different arena in which to listen and connect to the wants and desires of my body. I noticed that during chemo weeks, I couldn't do Pilates classes because it was harder to engage my core, but I loved to spin, walk and stretch. My week in between treatments, I craved more strength and power. Movement created an outlet for my mind and body, releasing mental fog, tension or congestion. To breathe and move makes me feel alive and appreciate the gift and power of my body.

What is your relationship to movement like? What type of movement does your body enjoy doing? How has your relationship to movement changed over time? What inspires you to move? How does your body communicate to you how it wants to move?

The tips that follow are ways you can add movement into your daily flow with gratitude and ease.

Move Your Body in Every Plane

We tend to move in the sagittal plane—moving only forward and backward. Try incorporating movements where your body twists, turns and moves side-to-side. Allow your body to explore the various dimensions.

Stairs Instead of Stagnant

Shift your perspective and keep your eyes out for stairs instead of elevators or escalators. Try to be conscious of where you can add more movement to your day. Remember, it is always a choice.

Digest to Rest

Take a walk after dinner to help your body digest so that you can have a restful sleep instead of feeling sluggish and bloated. It is a great time to connect to a partner, roommate, yourself, or catch up with a friend on the phone.

Posture Perfect

Great posture is not just about looking good and having a strong and confident appearance. Having great posture keeps your body aligned and creates space for your organs to do their thang. Be mindful of slouching over a computer or meal. Sit up straight by engaging your core and rolling your shoulders down your back.

Stretch It Out to Bust It Out

Start your morning with five minutes of basic stretching. Allow your body to unravel after a night's sleep by opening your chest, releasing your low back, lengthening your hamstrings and stretching your hips. Get the blood and breath flowing so you can feel alive, connected and engaged with your body.

Get Your Sweat On

Sweat it out at least twice a week to help clear your lymphatic system and flush toxins from your body. Know that you do not have to have an intense workout every day to be staying active and healthy, but a good sweat every so often is part of a balanced fitness routine.

Roll It Out

Grab a Yoga Tune Up® ball or tennis ball and roll out your feet. Notice how good it feels to release the fascia that tends to make your muscles feel restricted and your feet curl up. Help your feet stay grounded and fully connect to the earth as you walk.

Core Power

Strengthen your core to strengthen your presence. Feel connected to the mid-section of your body that helps you stand tall, strong and present. This is your powerhouse and it is the glue that connects your heart and legs. Try the classical Pilates hundreds exercise, Roll-ups or "Series of Five" for great feedback and strength building.

Switch It Up to Pump It Up

Don't get stuck in the same fitness routine. Mix up your schedule by adding a new weight routine, allowing a friend to introduce you to a new class, or challenging yourself to a new goal. Explore what happens when you step outside the routine.

Tunes to Improve

Let music wake up your body and mind to get going. Sometimes we can forget how lyrics to a song or a certain beat can be motivational to your heart. Pay attention to what type of music lights you up and helps pump you up to achieve that extra pull-up, run that last mile or feel that gentle stretch. Find the support and strength you want in music.

Walk It Out

Move your body, move your mind. Walk at least 20 minutes a day as part of your commute, exercise routine or for mid-day break. Notice how walking helps stimulate your mind, revives your creativity and gets your blood flowing. Research demonstrates walking boosts your immune system, curbs cravings, enhances your mood and improves overall health.

Find and Feel Your Alignment

At home or work, create better posture by standing against a wall to help you engage your core and lengthen your spine. Breathe into your rib cage as you hug your core to the wall. Stay here for three cycles of breath. Step away from the wall feeling taller and more connected.

Movement Game Plan

Create your movement game plan on Sundays before the busyness of the week gets hold of you. Sign up for fitness classes or physical activities and plug them into your schedule like meetings. Pick an accountability buddy if that helps, and make movement a part of your weekly ritual—a staple that doesn't get compromised. Check out these mindful movement practices on Centered in the City.

Make Fitness Fun

Staying active doesn't have to be painful. Choose three types of exercises you actually enjoy and help you feel strong and healthy. This way you are excited to move instead of dreading the process. Remember: it is how you feel, not how you look.

Fitness in Fresh Air

Let nature and fresh air inspire your body and lift your energy. Walk or bike to work, take a lunch break stroll or bring your mat to the park. Move your body in a natural setting and feel inspired in new ways.

Incline Your Booty

Walking is great, but if you are only walking on flat terrain, your booty isn't getting much attention. Find hills, stairs or steep driveways to bust out some power-walking to get your blood flowing, heart rate up and strengthen your back side. It's one of the best ways to counteract all of that sitting.

Accountability Is Key

Sick of going to the gym, taking the same classes or not being active at all? Sign up for a local charity race or triathlon to switch it up and help you create community around fitness. Joining a training team or working with a buddy helps you stay invested and supported so that you are more likely to stay committed to your mission.

Walking Is a Gateway Drug for Fitness

If you are new to the world of exercise, start small by adding more walking into your life. Once you get those endorphins flowing and feel more connected to your body, you will eventually crave more strength and cardio. Shift your mindset to 'just getting your steps in'. The rest will follow in time.

Sweaty Is Sexy

Get active with your partner, love interest or Tinder date--share a hike, run, yoga class or at-home YouTube session. When you sweat together, you release all sorts of hormones and endorphins that help to stimulate sexual chemistry. Not only are you supporting each other living a healthy lifestyle, but you are adding some spice to your relationship.

Bust a Move

Wind down from a busy day by blasting some jams and moving your booty in unexplored directions. Allow yourself to dance like no one is watching. Set your mind and body free while you decompress the day and come back to your center.

Space to Create
Your Own Mindful Moments

Journal Prompts — *Pick your practice.*

What *mindful moment* tip feels most aligned with your needs right now?

Why is practicing this tip important for you?

What about this tip gets you excited?

When do you want to commit to starting this practice? (Date, Time, Let's go!)

How do you imagine feeling while you practice this tip?

What is one tangible result you are hoping to create?

Pause to process.

What is one thing you are celebrating about yourself?

What stood out to you as you engaged with this practice?

How did this tip influence your energy, mood or mindset?

What's one insight you want to carry forward?

What are you grateful for in this moment?

With what do you surround yourself?

—

"Everything is energy

and that's all there is to it.

Match the frequency of the reality you want."

- Albert Einstein

Space

Pay attention to what you surround yourself with—from people to places, to objects and sensations. Notice how the energy inside and around you affects your overall well-being.

When you pay attention to your personal and shared spaces, you gain visual and physical cues that can guide and inspire you to live with more ease and energy.

The space with which you surround yourself can mean many things. It can mean physical spaces like your apartment, car, office, city, and overall environment aesthetic. But it also includes your personal space. For instance, who are you surrounded by? Who do you let into your personal space? They may be intimate relationships, friends, coworkers or family members. Sometimes you take your environment for granted, too; at least, I used to. I used to think, well that's just the way it is. These are the people in my life. This is where I live. This is what my room and house look like. And this is what life gets to look like. I never realized I had the power to be more intentional about what and with whom I surrounded myself until experiencing my "perfect storm." This awakening happened and deepened in stages.

At first, the importance of personal space, who I wanted around me became very apparent when my body and emotional energy were sensitive during chemotherapy and my mourning process. I had to cut out the friends who felt energetically draining to be around. I had to be conscious about creating space from them so I didn't feel weaker than I was. Instead, I surrounded myself with people who made me laugh, who could sit by my side and not say a word but just hold healing loving space; people who literally nourished my spirits. The impact of physical space became really apparent to me when New York City's energy became too much for my system to manage. The noise, the hustle and bustle, the schleping on crowded public transit became an extra load for me to handle. I did what I could do to make the environment more manageable. I would walk across Central Park as much as I could instead of taking the bus. I stayed in neighborhoods that were close and convenient. I consciously picked coffee shops that felt cozy to spend time in. Places where I could immerse myself in the solitary act of journaling, writing, or reading, while still finding comfort in the quiet presence of others.

My radar on what fueled me and what depleted me was on 'high sensitivity'. I knew that my body and spirit wanted to be back in Argentina. With a slower pace of living, warm people and a city full of palm trees and beautiful architecture, Argentina called me. The ability to tune in and think about who and what lifts me up and who and what depletes me is one of the most important navigational tools to remember. It all comes back to taking care of yourself and remembering that to set boundaries, to be clear or to make intentional choices isn't selfish. It is smart.

What impact do your physical spaces have on your well-being? How does your body feel in the current city or town you live in? Are you able to notice how different aesthetics of design makes you feel? Who in your life do you love to be around and feel your energy lift? What spaces make you feel most alive?

Here are some tips and tools to support you in thinking about your space.

One Hour Before Bedtime Is YOU Time

Turn off electronics, unplug from social media and allow yourself to
wind down from the day by creating a rejuvenating environment.
Dim the lights, play soothing music and light some aromatherapy candles
to help calm your nervous system.

Give Objects a Home

Everything you own gets to have a home. From shoes, to bags to jackets
and art supplies, designate a special space for each of your objects.
Mindfully place your stuff in the same spot every time you use it
to help reduce clutter.

Engage a Stranger

When commuting on public transit, standing in line at the coffee shop
or in an elevator, try stepping outside your world and asking someone how
they are? Mean it. Open your heart and allow yourself to connect—no matter
the outcome. Notice the positive energy you are spreading!

Energize Your Commute

Find one thing that inspires you on your way to work. It could be someone's
shoes, reading an interesting ad on the subway, listening to an inspiring
podcast or observing a sweet interaction between a group of people.
What was it that caught your attention? Bring that spark of curiosity
and awareness into your day.

Dust & De-clutter

Take a moment to examine your surroundings every time you leave
your environment; your car, bedroom, office or kitchen. Notice if you left
a cup, piece of garbage or papers lying around. Don't procrastinate tidying
up, instead, de-clutter your environment by removing at least one object that
makes you feel claustrophobic every time you transition from the space.

Awaken Your Space

Keep the energy in your apartment, home and desk alive with fresh flowers and plants. Remind yourself that life is always around and inside you. Find color, texture and life in your world.

Relationships Matter

Spend time with people that light you up versus bring you down. You are too precious to be around anyone that doesn't value who you are. Drop the baggage and emotional clutter to make room for people that matter.

Prevent Technology Fatigue

In moments where you find yourself waiting for a bus, elevator or stop sign, can you resist the urge to look at your phone? Don't allow your energy to be drained by the digital stimuli of texts or notifications; instead, gain energy from the beauty around you. Look up and out and notice your physical environment.

Unplug to Plug-in

Detach from electronics and the external world and take a moment to learn something about your internal world. Try winding down from your day by journaling for ten minutes. What can you learn about yourself that can help forward your humanness?

Light Up

Lighting profoundly impacts your productivity and energy levels. Think about how your space matches the task you want to do. Use softer and 'warmer' light (2700-3000K bulbs) to promote relaxation. Research demonstrates warmer lighting two-hours before bedtime helps improve sleep quality. Engage with 'cooler', whiter light (4000-5000K spectrum) to wake yourself up a bit.

Mirror Mirror on the Wall

Relationships get to be a reflection point. Sometimes we see something in others that we cannot see in ourselves. Take a moment to observe your relationships and notice how you interact in them. How do you communicate? Where do you find yourself getting annoyed? What ways do you give? What ways do you receive? Where does your curiosity come alive?

Daily Greens

Greens are not just meant to be eaten in your morning smoothie. They are meant to be seen and smelled as well. Spending time in nature helps to stimulate your mind, mood and overall sense of well-being. Get your daily greens in with a walk, reading in the park or just sitting on a bench observing. Being in nature helps to put all of life into perspective.

Passion Project

Create a hobby that lights you up and stimulates your soul. Incorporate that activity into your schedule so that you stay engaged with life outside of work and your lists of "to-dos." If you need help picking a project, ask yourself: "What did I like doing as a child?" Notice what ideas arise and how much more energized you will feel!

Create a Daily Adventure

From small to big to somewhere in between, create a daily adventure for yourself by simply switching up your commute, breaking a daily routine, eating at a new lunch spot or being spontaneous! Refresh your space so you can feel alive and present!

Scents

Scents have a huge psychological impact on how we interact with our environment. Rosemary stimulates your brain; bergamot, lavender and jasmine reduce anxiety; and cinnamon-vanilla stimulates creativity. Use candles, essential oils or natural air fresheners to help align yourself and your space together.

Fur Is In

Whether you are a big animal person or not, the science is right about the positive psychological effects our furry friends have on our nervous system. Spend some time with a furry friend to help feel at ease and relaxed. If you are allergic, looking at something cute and cuddly can also shift your energy and turn that frown upside down.

Teach Out to Reach In

Teach someone something today--a new word, something you learned on a podcast, read in an article or a skill that comes easily to you. Sharing your gifts and insights with others in your world creates an energetic exchange where you can savor the gift of connection.

Color Your World

We are all drawn to certain colors that make us feel calm, energized and inspired. Select colors and objects that support the mood and energy you want to feel. Think of your space as a blank canvas and the colors and textures you select get to inspire and light up your world.

Start with Your Sacred Space

Create an area in your apartment or house that feels healing, supportive, nurturing and that is only yours. Start your morning by entering into your physical sacred space so you can find your internal sacred space.

Savor the Moment

Don't take the little things for granted. Savor each bite, sight, conversation, sensation and sound. Slow down to feel the vibrations of what is around and inside of you. Don't let the fast-paced rhythm of the world make you skip a beat.

Space to Create
Your Own Mindful Moments

Journal Prompts — *Pick your practice.*

What *mindful moment* tip feels most aligned with your needs right now?

Why is practicing this tip important for you?

What about this tip gets you excited?

When do you want to commit to starting this practice? (Date, Time, Let's go!)

How do you imagine feeling while you practice this tip?

What is one tangible result you are hoping to create?

Pause to process.

What is one thing you are celebrating about yourself?

What stood out to you as you engaged with this practice?

How did this tip influence your energy, mood or mindset?

What's one insight you want to carry forward?

What are you grateful for in this moment?

How do you restore?

—

"The more light you allow within you, the brighter the world you live in will be."

- Shakti Gawain

Renewal

We are human-beings, not human-doings. In order to be productive, social, creative and intellectual individuals, there must be a balance to all the doing and going we create in our lives.

Renew your mind, body and soul with these tips to feel refreshed and rejuvenated.

Growing up in New York City, the idea of resting and slowing down is sort of an oxymoron. Only the "weak slow down" or "only those who can't keep up slow down" are some of the beliefs I grew up around. It wasn't until I lived in Buenos Aires the first time, I saw that it was possible to live in a hustling, bustling city, yet take time to enjoy the simple things in life like your coffee, or a conversation with a friend. When I came back to New York City to go through chemotherapy, I noticed I had no choice but to slow down and restore my energy. My body needed more sleep, my head needed more quiet time and my emotions needed more space.

Renewal is the tool to use for restoring your energy. It is the fuel that prevents your system from hitting burnout and running into the ground. Typically in America, we think renewal happens only a few times a year, when we can go on vacation. Whether you can afford to travel on vacation or have a stay-cation, the belief is that we can finally rest during those two weeks off. This culture ignores the daily moments and opportunities you have to renew and restore your energy. Such moments include your morning routine, transition moments, lunch breaks, and commutes. There are endless ways to practice slowing down and nourishing your energy levels.

I didn't connect to the concept of restoration until I was so low, my gas tank's light was on for months. Summer 2010 until 2012 felt like a marathon. I was not only experiencing bi-weekly chemotherapy treatments for six months, doctor appointments and scans, mourning my beloved mother, dealing with her estate, but I was working hard to finish college and to graduate from The University of Michigan on time.

Managing the uncertainty of life on this roller coaster ride for which I hadn't bought a ticket, taxed my system beyond belief. All I wanted to do was get healthy, graduate college and get back to Buenos Aires. When my dream manifested, I remember sitting on the beach in Punta Del Este, Uruguay, watching the sunset. I released a big sigh and felt tears run down my face. I made it back, I said to myself. I had a vision and I made it come true. I spent 10 days purely vegging on the beach-sleeping, reading, writing, working out, and people-watching. I had hit such a burnout that I needed to put some gas back in my vehicle just so that I could function.

After that experience, I promised myself I would try my hardest to not tax or over-burden my system. I learned how to manage my time and my schedule so I never felt like too much weight kept me down. I made conscious space to plan daily ways to renew my energy. Now, some of my favorite renewal practices are evening wind-downs in my sauna, sunrise mindful walks, journaling on my commute and my morning meditation ritual. All of these practices help keep me connected to me, my most valuable resource.

What is your relationship to rest? What are your favorite ways to renew your energy? How do you know when your well-being "gas tank" is nearing empty? What signs and signals do you want to pay attention to so that you can bring yourself back to homeostasis?

Explore how these tips create mindful space for you to renew your energy and connect you with you.

Sacred Time

Schedule at least 30 minutes of non-negotiable YOU time every day. Whether you wake up super early to receive it, take a break in the middle of your workday or stay up later, schedule in that self-care time. It gets to be filled with whatever you want, but only YOU get to decide and dictate.

Live Without a Schedule

Give yourself some freedom and space to live without your calendar. Agendas are great and all, but sometimes we need the unstructured play-time to feel young, liberated and alive. Find your natural rhythm by living in the space in between your commitments. Notice how you will feel refreshed and alive as you dis-engage from auto-pilot.

Go Nowhere. Be No One. Do Nothing.

Find a clutter-free space on your wall to lie on the ground and put your legs up the wall. Make sure your sit bones are close to where the wall and ground meet and let your mind and body go as you are held by the structure that surrounds you. Give your legs a break and give yourself permission to *be*. Breathe in deep and let the blood flow of your body renew your energy and perspective.

Get Dirty

Feel connected, relaxed and calm by getting your hands dirty in your garden. With a single plant in your apartment or in a big backyard, spend time tending to something living and green. Let the plant teach you patience as you watch nature.

Giving High

Nothing is more rewarding than giving back to your community. Through activities such as donating clothes, volunteering your time or organizing a fundraiser, you will discover ways you can connect and help serve your community. Supporting others not only becomes a positive force in your community, but that innate goodness seeps into your life. Research demonstrates volunteers live longer than non volunteers.

Take Five

Often all we need is five minutes to feel refreshed. When sitting in front of a computer, working on a group project or tapped into a video conference, see if you can step away for five minutes in order to take a breather. Restore your directed attention by taking a walk outside, meditating for a few minutes, doing jumping jacks or closing your eyes. Better yet, buffer in 5 minute breaks in your calendar between meetings to reset.

Let it Go to Let it Flow

In order to feel energized and restored, you sometimes have to let shit go to get back into your flow. Letting emotions and thoughts go can feel sticky and stubborn. Try connecting to your breath and let every inhale and exhale purify your system. Imagine each thought or sensation as a leaf that you can let go of and blow into the wind.

The Three Bs

Wind down from a busy and chaotic day with my "Three Bs." Put your favorite tunes on and bust a move with some kickass **B**eats. **B**oil water to enjoy some soothing tea. And run a bubble **B**ath to help physically melt away the stress of the day. Notice how your energy shifts when you can let the adrenaline drift away.

Take Yourself on a Date

Life can get busy, but don't forget to take yourself out on a date and re-connect. Treat yourself to a mani pedi, a delicious meal out, a solo vacation or a cozy night in to read a book. Spending time alone is healing and grounding.

Clean Your Brain

Sleep is one of the most powerful tools to clean and clear the plaque buildup in your brain—literally and physiologically. Get your nightly rest to practice mental hygiene so you can stay clean, fresh and sharp during your day.

Practice the Transitions

When you arrive home, create a ritual that helps you transition from your outside world into your restorative space. Consider sitting on the couch for a few minutes, drinking a glass of water or snuggling with your dog—take a moment to pause and fully transition from your go-go-go pace to slowing down to relaxing at home. Let this ritual spark your desire to wind down.

Creative Time

Express yourself in any form! Painting, cooking, dancing, making a gift or scrap-booking—tap into your creative side. Forming daily or weekly creative dates with yourself and others is a great way to restore your energy.

Innocent Playtime

Tap into your inner child and play without a care, rule, guideline or restriction in the world. Resist the urge to have your adult mind place expectations or judgments on the event. Softening the adult mind helps to reduce the weight of responsibility so you can feel at ease and be detached from the outcome.

Spa Day

Five-star spa or not, you can always create a spa day in your very own home. Use aromatherapy, candles, creams, face masks, incense, bubble bath, epsom salts, face-masks and yummy lotions to help hydrate and pamper yourself from the outside in. Renew your soul with smells of lavender, jasmine and rose. Melt into smooth and soft textures and be lulled to sleep with soothing music and dim light.

Be Lazy

How often do you give yourself permission to be lazy? The type of lazy where you linger in bed longer than you think you should. Sometimes there is a tendency to feel guilty in our culture for not being productive. However, here is your permission to be lazy if that's what feels good! You get to discern for yourself. You deserve a day to detach and unplug from everything, including social pressures.

Make Yourself Your #1 Priority by Saying NO

Remember you are the constant in every scenario you are in. It's not selfish to care for yourself by putting your own oxygen mask on first. Practice saying no when your body tells you something is a "yuck" versus a "yum." Saying no helps you restore your batteries so that you have energy when you want to say yes.

Talk to Your Soul

In moments of intense emotions or unsettled thoughts, turn to your journal to process and reset. Take time to reveal, heal and de-clutter what is making you feel your truth in the moment. Ask yourself, "what's true for me at this moment?" Notice what you feel when you can process the emotions instead of burying them.

Give Your Feet Some Lovin'

Wind down after a busy day with a foot massage. Either rub your own feet as an act of self-love or massage your partner's or roommate's as a great way to connect and catch up on each other's day. Notice how good it feels to give your feet some attention and love while taking the time to talk and listen.

QT

Sometimes all you need is a little bit of TLC to feel refreshed. Instead of looking to the external world, turn into yourself. Curl up with a cozy book, a funny movie, your journal or your pet, and give yourself some quiet time to feel restored. Quiet time isn't punishment—it is a healing way to neutralize your daily experiences.

Listen More

Notice if your natural tendency is to "do" and fill silence with your thoughts, words or gestures. Find the deeper meaning in silence by resting back and listening more closely. Whether you are having an actual conversation with a friend or spending solo time at a coffee shop, listening is an easeful way to connect more deeply.

Space to Create
Your Own Mindful Moments

_____

_____

_____

_____

_____

_____

_____

_____

_____

_____

_____

_____

_____

_____

_____

_____

_____

_____

_____

_____

_____

_____

_____

_____

_____

Journal Prompts — *Pick your practice.*

What *mindful moment* tip feels most aligned with your needs right now?

Why is practicing this tip important for you?

What about this tip gets you excited?

When do you want to commit to starting this practice? (Date, Time, Let's go!)

How do you imagine feeling while you practice this tip?

What is one tangible result you are hoping to create?

Pause to process.

What is one thing you are celebrating about yourself?

What stood out to you as you engaged with this practice?

How did this tip influence your energy, mood or mindset?

What's one insight you want to carry forward?

What are you grateful for in this moment?

Dedication of Merit

*May the care and presence cultivated through
this book ripple outward, supporting your well-being
and the world around you.*

*May you remember that self-care is not selfish,
but a foundation for greater love and compassion.*

As you take care, may it inspire others to do the same.

*And may this practice bring happiness, health,
and freedom to all beings.*

With gratitude, may our practices be of benefit.

About Wade Brill

Faced with multiple life interruptions before the age of 21, Wade Brill learned the value of each day and the importance to live an authentic, fulfilled and healthy life. Wade's major life interruptions included divorced parents, three family cancer episodes (her mother, sister and herself), losing her mother to cancer while they both were in cancer treatment, moving to a different country, and starting her own businesses.

Life is short. Wade knows this intimately and is passionate about helping others take care of themselves from the inside out. She believes that when you prioritize taking care of yourself, you are then able to show up full-heartedly in the world and vibrate inspiring energy to the world.

Wade was born and raised in the energetic hustle and bustle of Manhattan. She attended the University of Michigan where she received her B.A. in American Culture. After college, she followed the urge to move back to Buenos Aires–a city she first fell in love with while studying abroad. Wade planted roots while running her own Pilates and meditation business. Helping people feel physically fit was rewarding, but Wade always wanted to help people feel mentally and emotionally fit as well. She moved to the other side of the world, Seattle, with the gringo love of her life and became a Professional Certified Mindfulness Coach.

In 2015, Wade co-founded *Centered in the City*, a pioneering coaching collective that seamlessly integrates mindfulness, self-development, and authentic connection. Through weekly meditation sessions, community-driven social events, and energy-based self-development workshops, Wade cultivated a supportive space for individuals to pause, reflect, and grow. The initiative evolved into a dynamic ecosystem, including the *Centered in the City* podcast and an innovative virtual platform offering on-demand mindfulness and self-care resources.

This platform empowers busy professionals to "get centered" and navigate the demands of modern life with greater ease and presence.

Wade's expertise extends to corporate leadership trainings for Fortune 500 companies, where she emphasizes the transformative power of resilience training, stress management strategies, and mindful communication. Her work equips organizations with tools to enhance well-being, foster trust, and boost productivity.

A passionate advocate for personal transformation, Wade works closely with high-achieving individuals, helping them manage overwhelm and cultivate a sense of calm, confidence, and alignment in their lives. She also leads impactful workshops and retreats worldwide, guiding participants to reconnect with their center and deepen their self-awareness.

Wade's contributions to the field of mindfulness are recognized through her role as a board member of the International Mindfulness Teachers Association, where she continues to advance the integration of mindfulness into everyday life and work.

Stay Connected!

Thank you from the bottom of my heart for being here and honoring your life and well-being. By you carrying for your holistic self, may this work continue to ripple into the world and be of service and benefit to all beings.

If you found this book helpful, please consider sharing it with a friend. May we all be empowered to care for ourselves so that we can show up for one another with an open heart and do good for the greater world.

Join my free newsletter: **www.wadebrill.com/get-centered**
Connect via Instagram: **@OneWade**
Send me a note: **WadeBrill.com/connect**

Listen to the Centered in the City podcast:
https://tinyurl.com/centeredinthecity

Enjoy mindfulness and self-care practices:
https://www.centeredinthecity.org/centeredspace

Learn more about coaching engagements here:
https://wadebrill.com/individualcoaching

Book me for speaking and facilitation engagements here:
https://www.wadebrill.com/speaking

Besos,
Wade.

www.ingramcontent.com/pod-product-compliance
Lightning Source LLC
Chambersburg PA
CBHW040904120626
46551CB00006B/637

* 9 7 9 8 9 9 2 8 8 6 8 0 1 *